The Practice of No Problem

A Deceptively Simple Approach to Profound Meditation

Jeff Carreira

The Practice of No Problem
A Deceptively Simple Approach to Profound Meditation
By Jeff Carreira

Copyright © 2014
Emergence Education & Jeff Carreira

ISBN-13: 978-0615996585 (Emergence Education)
ISBN-10: 0615996582

Emergence Education
230 Stampers Street
Philadelphia, PA 01947

Cover design by www.choosefreeagency.com

How do you meditate?

Close your eyes and Surrender.

—Rumi

CONTENTS

The soul should always stand ajar, ready to welcome the ecstatic experience.

—Emily Dickinson

INTRODUCTION

You are about to embark on a journey.

This book is an exploration of the four most valuable insights that my own meditation practice has blessed me with. These insights are an invitation to the profound possibility of inner freedom. Following them carefully will support your own ongoing process of awakening.

The first chapter introduces the foundational premise upon which the remainder of the book rests—meditation can initiate a process of profound spiritual transformation. The second chapter details an approach to the practice of meditation based on the conscious embrace of having no problem, a practice that is both simple and profound. Each of the remaining four chapters is dedicated to one of the most profound insights that I have gained through my many years of meditative experience.

This book is meant to take you somewhere. I suggest that you read it carefully in small bits that give you time to orient yourself in the direction it points. Don't be overly concerned with understanding, allow yourself to be taken to where the book invites you.

Before we begin this journey consider the fact that this book can only take you as far as you are ready to go. How much you experience will be largely dependent on how much room you have in your heart for the miraculous.

No matter what your mind might say, you actually don't know what can happen during the reading of this book. It's possible that you will have an opening that dramatically impacts your life. You might even have an insight that changes the course of your destiny and places you on a new and magnificent trajectory. I know this is possible because it has happened to me and I have seen it happen for others.

Take a moment to notice whether you experience excitement and inspiration, or resistance and doubt in relationship to this possibility.

You don't need to do anything with your response. Just being aware of it is enough. Then read the book, give it all of your attention, and see what happens.

I've begun to realize that you can listen to silence and learn from it. It has a quality and a dimension all its own.

—Chaim Potok

CHAPTER ONE

MEDITATION AND TRANSFORMATION

I have dedicated my life to the exploration of the profound potential for transformation that all human beings possess. In this pursuit I have had the grace of experiencing transformation at the core of my being and I have always had other pioneering souls with whom to share and explore with. All of that experience has brought with it an unshakeable conviction that there is a profound relationship between meditation and transformation. In this chapter I share my understanding of how and why the experience of meditation profoundly enhances our capacity to transform.

Let me be clear that when I talk about meditation I am not referring only to sitting with your eyes closed. I am talking about deep abidance in the experience of who we are beyond the mind. The posture or form that initiates that abidance doesn't ultimately matter. All that matters is that we move beyond the assumed limits of the mind.

You see, our minds have been profoundly conditioned to remain relentlessly fixated on a certain range of thoughts, feelings, and sensory perceptions that actually lie within a much larger field of awareness. Because this range is what we have become habituated to perceive, we assume that it is all there is to be aware of. One of the miracles of meditation is the discovery that we can perceive more than our minds can. In fact, we are already conscious of more than our minds can know.

Meditation—whether it's done sitting with your eyes closed or using some other method—occurs when you discover how to remove your attention from anything in particular and allow it to float freely in consciousness.

When meditation occurs it is like realizing that you can fly. You live your whole life anchored to a narrow range of thoughts, feelings and sensations, and suddenly you find yourself floating in midair. Nothing is more exhilarating or mind altering than the freedom you find in true meditation.

To understand the relationship between meditation and transformation the first thing we have to realize is that the entirety of our current experience of being human has been carved out of a much vaster field of possible experience.

We know that our eyes only perceive a narrow part of the electro-magnetic spectrum, and our ears only hear a small range of sound frequencies. In the same way our minds only experience a small part of an immeasurable field of consciousness.

As I already stated, one of the great miracles that can be discovered through meditation is that we have the ability to experience consciousness beyond what the mind is capable of experiencing. We are not our minds and our ability to experience is not limited by our minds. This discovery is like seeing beyond what the eye can see, or hearing more than what the ear can hear. We have much more access to consciousness than what the mind alone experiences.

The next thing that we have to realize in order to fully appreciate the relationship between meditation and transformation is that all of reality is in constant flux. We are born into an unintelligible rush of experience.

Slowly we learn how to filter our perception so that we stabilize in a particular experience of being someone. Within an unceasing flow of experience we have temporarily stabilized into the experience of being 'me.' By ceaselessly focusing on a limited part of the ever shifting field of experience we are able to experience ourselves as a static being.

In order to stabilize into a particular identity we had to learn to remain doggedly fixated on a narrow band of consciousness—the experience of being 'me.' That habit of riveting our attention on the experience of being me is so strong that we have forgotten that there is any other possibility. Most people live their lives, busy being whoever they learned to be in the first place.

Some of us become interested in transformation. We begin to feel stifled by the fixed sense of self that we are. We begin to realize that we are more than that, but we don't know how to break the habit of mental fixation that holds our identity in place.

If we want to transform, if we want to expand our experience of consciousness and identity, we have to first unglue our attention from the small band of possibility that we have become habitually adhered to. Meditation is a practice for releasing our awareness.

The experience of freedom is the first miracle of meditation. The second is the discovery that once our attention has been liberated from strict adherence to our current sense of self we are available to enter into a natural process of growth.

Once we discover the miracle of free-floating consciousness we begin to realize something even more miraculous. Consciousness naturally expands.

The transformation of consciousness is what we experience as soon as we stop holding ourselves to only one spot in consciousness.

Suddenly it all makes sense. Growth is a natural part of life. Everything grows and often without much force or effort. Trees don't have to force themselves to grow from seed to maturity, nor do flowers or animals or birds. Growth is the essence of being alive.

Why wouldn't consciousness grow in the same way?

As we enter into a more natural process of growth we realize that we have been holding on to who we are at the very same time that we have been trying to change. Pushing off of the past is just another way of holding on to it. The experience of meditation is the experience of letting go of who we are. And as soon as we let go of who we are, we enter a natural process of growth and evolution.

Deep meditation allows us to let go of who we habitually think we are and frees us to become more than that. That is why I see it as an essential part of the transformative process.

Give up the notion that 'I am so and so.'
All that is required to realize the Self is
to be still. What can be easier than that?

—Ramana Maharshi

CHAPTER TWO

THE PRACTICE OF HAVING NO PROBLEM

The meditation practice that I am introducing is the simplest thing you can possibly do. In fact it is so simple that you are already doing it right now without realizing it. You have been doing it for as long as you've been alive and will continue until the day you die. In fact, I believe that you were doing it before you were born, and will continue after you die.

The meditation instructions that I will share cannot be done wrong. You literally can't miss. That is why I sometimes describe them as a magic archery range.

The magic archery range has no targets. You just shoot an arrow in any direction and wherever you aim a target appears and you hit a bull's eye...every time. It's an archery range where you can't miss. That's the magic.

What we discover in the magic archery range, is that only when we are in a situation where we can't lose, do we have the opportunity to see how difficult it can be to always win. That is because our mind is a problem-solving machine, and it will create a problem out of anything—even not being able to lose.

As you approach this form of meditation you have to consider if you are ready to live a life where you can't miss, if you are truly ready to be content, and if you are ready to give up the luxury of having a problem to escape into.

It is an important contemplation because until you are ready to have no problem you will continue to make problems for yourself. As soon as you're ready to have no problem you will discover a new world.

The instruction for this meditation is simply to have no problem. You sit still, upright and alert, and no matter what you experience, you don't make a problem out of it. There is nothing else to it.

No matter what you experience don't make a problem out of it. Even if your mind tells you that you have a problem, don't have a problem with that. If you feel like you have a problem, don't have a problem with that. If everything in you is saying you have a problem, don't have a problem with that either.

It is a tremendously easy meditation to do for a short amount of time. When the time gets longer we find out how hard it can be to have no problem.

You can try it right now. Time yourself for five seconds while you sit still and follow the instruction to have no problem.

Having no problem is easy for five seconds because your mind doesn't have enough time to even start looking for a problem. As you extend the time it gets more difficult.

If you are successful, eventually you will discover something miraculous. You will realize that you don't have to have a problem even if your mind does. When you realize this you will discover a profound degree of freedom from self-concern.

When you sit in meditation and your only instruction is to have no problem, one of the problems your mind will tend to create is that you don't know what to focus on. "What do I focus on?" your mind will ask. And then it will probably start arguing that not having a focus is a big problem.

No matter what problem your mind creates, you will find that it always comes in the form of an argument your mind is making to convince you that there is a problem. In this case it might go like this: "What am I supposed to focus on? He didn't tell me what to focus on. I don't know what to focus on. This is not fair. It won't work. I can't do this. It can't be done because there is nothing to focus on."

That is not a problem. It is just a conversation happening in your mind. And that conversation, no matter what form it takes, does not have to be a problem.

Have you ever had a friend that complains all the time? No matter what happens, they always seem to find a problem to complain about. For a while, you might talk to them about their problems. But eventually it gets exhausting. After a while you don't want to be involved with their problems. Your mind is a little like that friend. It always has a problem, and after a while it gets exhausting.

Of course, sometimes your mind is your best friend. We all want to use our mind for the things it does best, but we don't want to get involved with all of its problems.

With your friend there are times when you just decide not to listen to them. They may even keep talking to you. But you're not really listening anymore. The same thing can happen with your mind. It'll keep saying, "I don't know what to focus on. I don't know what to focus on. I don't know what to focus on." And you just sit there.

It's like a radio playing in the next room. You hear the sound, but you're not listening.

Every problem you will ever have in meditation will always be a conversation that your mind is having with you. All you have to do is not listen to it, and then you're free. Eventually, your mind gets bored and stops talking, and that can be wonderful, but it doesn't matter. The point is that we don't have to wait for our mind to stop talking before we stop listening.

We might assume that once we decide to have no relationship to our thoughts and problems, that they will stop, but they don't. Imagine driving a car down the highway with your foot on the gas. You may decide to take your foot off the gas, but that does not mean the car will stop. It keeps going. Just like your mind. You may decide to stop giving it your attention, but that doesn't make it stop.

It takes time for your mind to stop because it has a lot of momentum behind it. But that is not a problem. You just let it go. It will coast to a stop eventually, and if it doesn't, who cares? It isn't hurting anything. It isn't doing anything. It can't touch you. So you're free anyway.

One of the tricky things about the practice of no problem is that it has to be done all at once. There is no gradual way to approach it. You have to decide that from this moment forward you will not allow yourself to relate to anything as a problem—at least during meditation. From that point on you simply adopt the position that nothing is a problem—no matter what. Simple.

What often happens is that we keep catching ourselves in the middle of believing that there is something wrong and then bringing ourselves back to the recognition that nothing is wrong. Unfortunately the very act of bringing ourselves back implies that there was something wrong with wherever we were.

It is easy for this meditation practice to become all about remembering that there is no problem. But the practice is not about remembering that there is no problem; it is about having no problem. So we need to be able to have no problem with the fact that we forget and fall back into having a problem.

So what do you do when you realize that you have been lost in having a problem? Nothing. Once you realize that you were lost, you aren't lost anymore and so there is nothing you have to do except have no problem with having been lost.

Every problem is just another voice in your head telling you that you have a problem. Those voices are often followed by other voices that tell you not to listen to that voice. Then other voices might start having a problem with all the voices. "You shouldn't be thinking. You're not supposed to be thinking. You're not really doing it. I knew you couldn't do it. You'll never be able to do it." Sound familiar?

Eventually, you realize that every problem is just another voice in your head telling you that you have a problem. When you realize that those voices are not you, that you are the one who hears the voices, something completely different happens. At that point you stop caring about what any of the voices are saying. The voices may fall away, or they may not. It doesn't matter to you because you are free either way.

I once had the opportunity to do a meditation retreat for two months. I was meditating from four in the morning until ten at night. I had always had difficulty with falling asleep in meditation and during this retreat I was determined not to fall asleep.

One day at the beginning of the second month, I was meditating and I was very tired. It can be almost torturous to meditate when you're very tired. Your eyes burn, your head hurts, and you feel nervous tension running through your body.

As I was sitting in this very difficult situation a thought went through my mind. It said, "You're not really tired." And for some reason in that instant something profound happened, I realized that I wasn't tired. I just happened to be looking through a tired body, but I was completely awake anyway. In fact I had never been other than completely awake. It is not possible to be less than completely awake.

Awareness is always on, and there is no dimmer switch. You can't turn it down. Sometimes what you are aware of is a very tired body, but no matter what happens, you are always awake, even if what you are awake to is being tired.

When I went to sleep that night, I felt my body fall asleep but I was still there. Everything went black and I couldn't feel my body. I was just floating in space. I thought, "This is cool. My body fell asleep and I'm still awake."

Then a dream happened. It was like someone turned the lights on and I was in the middle of a dream. I thought, "I am dreaming and I am still awake. This is so cool." Then the dream went away as if the light had been turned off again. There I was floating in space.

Then another dream appeared and disappeared. Then another. When my alarm went off in the morning my body woke up and I thought, " I'm still here." I started to wonder, Who was asleep? Who is awake now? And what is the difference between meditating and just walking around if I am here all the time anyway.

The next night, the same thing happened. My body fell asleep and I was still here. I thought, "Oh, this is cool." And I spent the whole next day marveling at the fact that I am always here. I am always awake. The next night my body fell asleep and I remained awake again. Then I started to worry that this might not be healthy and the next night I fell asleep and I lost consciousness. When I woke up in the morning I was relieved at first and then disappointed.

What I realized from that experience will stay with me forever. We are always awake no matter how it seems. We were awake before we were born, and we will continue to be awake after we die. Whether we are aware of it or not in any given moment doesn't matter. It is still true even when we don't realize it.

The practice of no problem is about being with everything exactly the way it already is. Most of us live in a struggle with the way things are. As long as our energy is wrapped up in a struggle with the way things are, we are not available for anything more. As long as we are locked in a struggle nothing changes.

If you learn to accept the way things are your energy is free, your attention is free, and you are available to experience things that you couldn't imagine before. That is when you become profoundly available to evolve. When we learn to stop struggling with the way things are, we are available to be lifted into higher possibilities.

I, I myself, am the center that exists only because the geometry of the abyss demands it.

—Fernando Pessoa

CHAPTER THREE

FIRST INSIGHT:
LIBERATION IS POSSIBLE

The first insight that I want to share tells us that spiritual awakening depends on the fact that we know in our heart of hearts that liberation is possible. We all come to the spiritual path called by a possibility. In some way we have felt limited and we knew that limitation was not real. Usually, we discover this because of some experience, some recognition, or some insight that revealed something else—an unlimited, unbounded possibility.

In the light of that insight or experience or realization, our normal relationship to the world and to ourselves feels like it is stuffed into a box much too small to reflect reality. So we embark on a spiritual path.

The key to attaining the awakening that we seek is knowing that it is possible. In your heart of hearts, you must already know that it's possible. And even more you must know that it is possible now.

Thinking that it is possible in the future, even being certain that awakening is possible in the future, is still predicated on an assumption that it is not possible now. If I owe you money and you say, "Are you going to pay me the money?" and I say, "I will definitely pay you tomorrow." What I am also saying is, "I am not going to pay you now."

So, if you say, "I know that I can be free tomorrow. I know that liberation will be possible tomorrow or at some point in the future, even a few seconds from now." You're also saying, "I know it's not possible now."

The journey that we are on together here has to start at the deep end of the pool because the beginning of this journey is knowing that liberation is possible right now for all of us. This is a journey that starts at the destination. You don't find liberation, you realize that it was always here.

Take a moment to scan your experience. Whatever you are experiencing right now, whatever thoughts you are having, whatever you are looking at, whatever your body feels like, whatever emotions might be arising, whatever it is, has to be what liberation is, because otherwise it would not be available until your experience changed.

The only place that you can find freedom is right here. Right here in the middle of the experience you're already having. This is where freedom exists. It doesn't exist anywhere else. It doesn't exist in some future moment. It doesn't exist in some memory of the past.

Right now, in the experience that you're currently having, freedom already is. The fact that you may or may not feel free does not in any way limit the possibility of being free now. Liberation has to be available right now and not an instant later.

My intention in writing this book is to bring you to the direct recognition that you are already always free, that you always have been already free, and always will be.

The key to recognizing and experiencing and becoming aware of your own liberation is knowing beyond doubt that nothing that you are experiencing right now disqualifies this moment from being a moment of freedom. Freedom is here no matter what your mind might be telling you, no matter how many excuses it might be throwing at you.

"No, this couldn't be it. This can't be liberation. Liberation can't include this feeling. Liberation can't include this experience. Liberation can't include this thought."

There will always be a part of us that continuously attempts to disqualify this moment, which is the only moment there is, from being the one. It will always find a way to try to convince you that this could not possibly be the moment, that liberation is not possible right now.

And that part of us will always conclude that something needs to change—some feeling needs to be included or some other feeling excluded, some thought needs to be extricated or some other thought needs to be found. Whatever it is, that part of you will always believe that the experience of this moment requires some amount of tinkering, shifting, altering, or tweaking before freedom will be possible.

Ultimately, the only thing that keeps us from recognizing our inherently liberated state is our belief in some excuse that is trying to convince us that freedom isn't possible yet. If we believe that justification, we won't feel free and we won't believe that freedom is here. Instead we will feel as though we are stuck in a moment that isn't the right moment, and feel trapped in an experience that is not free.

If we don't believe that part of our mind we discover that even the thoughts that are trying to convince us that this is not the moment, are themselves just thoughts that don't in any way inhibit the possibility of freedom now. We immediately realize that we do not know what is possible and that means that anything is possible right now. And when we feel that anything is possible right now, that's as free as we can be.

Mysticism is the art of union with Reality.

—Evelyn Underhill

CHAPTER 4

SECOND INSIGHT:
LIBERATION IS ALREADY YOURS

You might be able to tell by the title of this chapter that we already began the exploration of this insight in the last chapter. In this book I am sharing with you the most powerful insights that my meditation practice has blessed me with. In fact, it is probably more accurate to think of these four insights as different entry points into one profoundly liberating insight. It is not a new insight by any means. In fact you will find it in spiritual traditions the world over. In one form or another that insight always tells us that what we seek is already ours.

The first insight is that spiritual awakening depends on the fact that we know in our heart of hearts without doubt that liberation is possible *now*. Now we will go further into this realization by exploring an insight that tells us that liberation is already ours.

Once we know that liberation is already here. Once we know that liberation is already possible, then there's nothing left to do other than accept that fact. In the context of meditation, liberation is simply the state of being exactly here in the present moment where nothing is missing, nothing is wrong, nothing needs to change, and nothing needs to be different than it is. There is no tension around needing to be anywhere other than here or needing anything to be anything other than what it already is.

When I say that liberation is already yours, I mean that there is already a place in your being, a part of your current experience, that is completely at peace with the way things are, completely at one with whatever arises in the present moment, and already has no need for anything to be other than what it is.

This insight is crucial because it completely changes our relationship to meditation. It is easy when we meditate to consciously or unconsciously assume that we need to go someplace other than here in order to be free.

When we realize that there is a part of us that is always already free, and that always already exists in this moment, as freedom, then we realize that the only place that freedom can be found is here. The only place that perfect contentment can be found is here.

There is a part of you that will never feel perfectly content. No matter what happens and no matter what your experience is, part of you will experience whatever is happening as somehow wrong, deficient, or simply "not it." If your attention is on this sense of deficiency in yourself, then you will not experience perfect contentment.

And here is the whole point: The fact that you may have your attention on the part of your experience that will never be contentment doesn't mean that some other place in your being, some other part of your experience, isn't already perfectly content now.

The practice of meditation is not a practice of changing your experience. It's not a movement from an experience that is "not it" toward some other experience that is. It is not any altering of the experience you're having so that it can become the experience of freedom. It is simply allowing yourself to know that perfect contentment is already yours even if your attention happens to be somewhere else. Even if your attention is on a part of yourself that feels discontent, unsettled, unresolved, incomplete, uncomfortable, or whatever else it might be, freedom and perfect contentment are already yours.

There is a part of you that has always been free, has always been content, and has always been at peace with the way things are—even with the fact that your attention is often captivated by a part of your experience that is not at peace.

The movement of meditation is not a movement from one consciousness to another, or even a movement from one place in consciousness to another. Meditation is an acceptance of the totality of who you already are regardless of what your experience might be.

Freedom is literally already here. This is so hard to truly get that it will be a theme that we return to over and over again throughout the rest of this book. The liberation you seek, the freedom you seek, the contentment you seek is already here no matter how it seems. There is no reason to try to understand that. There is no reason to try to convince yourself of the truth of it. Your mind will probably never accept it. It is true anyway.

You simply surrender to the reality of it and then see what happens. You place no demands that your experience needs to shift. Whatever you're experiencing right now, whatever it is, does not need to change one single bit. Freedom is just as available in the experience you're having right now as it is in any other possible experience you could be having. Freedom is always completely available. All we have to do is be available to it.

Perfect contentment is always already yours regardless of what you're experiencing and regardless of what your attention may be focused on at any given moment.

The reality that can be so difficult for us to accept is that freedom is already ours. There is no reality other than the one we are already in. There is no place to go and nothing you need to do with the experience you are having right now, even with this feeling, even with that thought, even with this experience, even with that, and even with anything else that might possibly arise.

None of it makes freedom any less available because a part of you is already free, already perfectly content. Meditation is just an expansion into the totality of who you already are.

We are so conditioned and so trained to limit who we are by the sphere of what we happen to be consciously aware of. It's like being in a darkened room, using only a narrow flashlight beam to see by, and thinking that the only things that exist in that room are what that thin beam can illuminate. We assume that nothing exists out beyond the edges of the light.

But the part of your experience that happens to be illuminated by the light of your conscious attention is not the whole of your experience.

Your experience extends way beyond the edges of your conscious attention.

If the experience that is currently illuminated by the light of your conscious attention is not one of freedom and contentment, that doesn't mean that freedom and contentment are not already yours. It doesn't mean that freedom and contentment aren't already a part of your experience.

Just because the flashlight beam in the darkened room happens to be illuminating only one wall doesn't mean that the others aren't there.

When you discover the freedom that exists outside of the bounds of your conscious awareness you stop needing to manipulate your conscious awareness. You know that freedom is already there and so you don't feel any need to locate it to be certain. It is like knowing that the sun is still there on a cloudy day. You never fear that the sun is gone. You know it is there and it will return into view when the clouds part. The discovery of true freedom doesn't mean that you will always feel free, but you will never forget that you are.

Liberation will always be yours once you realize that there is a part of your experience that is, was, and will always be free, even if it exists beyond the bounds of your conscious awareness. In this realization you realize that freedom and contentment is always already yours.

At that point, which is now, you are free from any need to have your experience be anything other than what it is because you are already free and content, totally awake and aware anyway. You realize that your experience expands far beyond the illuminating light of your conscious awareness. You relax into the totality of your being, needing to do nothing, needing to go nowhere. Then the miraculous reality of who you are has the opportunity to unfold in whatever way it will.

I firmly disbelieve, myself, that our human experience is the highest form of experience existent in the universe.

—William James

CHAPTER 5

THIRD INSIGHT:
LIBERATION IS MORE THAN A FEELING

The insight that we will explore now tells us that liberation is more than a feeling. In order to fully accept that liberation is already ours we have to find a way to embrace a freedom that exists outside of the sphere of our conscious awareness and is not limited by how we happen to feel.

That means we have to accept that perfect contentment is already part of our experience, even though it may not be inside of our conscious awareness. The challenge of this insight is to embrace the reality of an experience that lies outside of what we have been conditioned to perceive, and how we have learned to define ourselves.

Freedom is the perfect peace that comes when we are completely content being exactly who and where we are, with no need or desire for things to be any other way. The central message of this book and the recognition that the practice of no problem leads to, is that liberation already exists as part of who you are—which is ultimately why there is no problem.

When we insist that freedom must be part of our consciously held experience before we are willing to acknowledge its existence, what we are saying is that we are only free when we feel free. Only when the feeling of liberation appears in our conscious sphere of awareness do we recognize it. We are in essence insisting that freedom only exists when we are consciously aware of it. This insistence is so subtle that it is easily missed and as many times as we see beyond it, it returns in an even more subtle form to deceive us again.

We all live under the spell of a pervasive assumption that we are only free when we feel free, but a moment's reflection will confirm that if you are only free when you feel free, you cannot be free. You are bound by the need to feel free. To go back to our analogy of a darkened room, it is like saying that a particular piece of furniture only exists if it is illuminated by the beam of the flashlight. If I don't see it, if it lies in the darkness, it doesn't exist for me.

As long as we are consciously or unconsciously holding that relationship to freedom we will be forever trying to find some feeling of being free. We will feel that we must manipulate our conscious sphere of awareness so that somehow a feeling of liberation always remains within its borders. The only time we will be free is when we feel free. Otherwise we will be in a constant struggle with the way things are; trapped by the need to feel free.

When we accept, as we have been exploring already, that freedom always exists as part of our being even if it is outside of our normal sphere of conscious awareness, then we no longer demand that our experience has to change in order for us to be free. This acceptance allows us to look for freedom inside of the experience that we are already having in this moment. It invites us to stop looking outside of the experience of this moment to find liberation and instead to look beyond the edges of our conscious awareness toward the freedom that exists already just beyond what we can see. Rather than manufacturing freedom or going somewhere else to find it we allow our attention to expand and extend beyond the borders of our normal sphere of awareness. What we discover is that freedom can always be found beyond the edges of our mind.

This discovery dissolves all tension. There is no fear of failure because I already know that freedom is here. There is no need to experience it or to 'see' it in order to know that it is here. This recognition is the source of true spiritual liberation. We no longer need to see or experience a feeling of freedom in order to be completely assured that it is already here.

By liberating ourselves from the compulsive need to *feel* free in order to *be* free, we become available for a natural expansion of consciousness that is always waiting for us.

We are coming full circle to where we started. We began this exploration by saying that in order for spiritual awakening to be possible, we have to know in our heart of hearts that it is, indeed, possible. We have to know that it is possible to be free now. For freedom to be possible now it must already exist now. If freedom is not already here it would have to take some amount of time, however small, to get to wherever it is, or to bring it here. Any belief that there is some place we have to go, or something we have to do, before we can be free, means we are still convinced that freedom does not already exist here and now.

The first insight told us that our liberation depends on our knowing that liberation is possible now. As we come back to that insight we realize that it requires us to give up any insistence that our experience confirms our freedom. To be free we have to stop demanding proof. We have to know that freedom is already here regardless of how we feel. We must be certain that illumination already exists in our being, even when it is not within our current conscious sphere of awareness.

Then we can finally relax into reality exactly as it is, because there is nothing wrong, there is nothing to become, and there is no need to go anywhere. We simply expand into the fullness of who we already are.

The practice of meditation is not designed to transform us into someone other than who we already are. Meditation allows us to become the fullness of who we are already.

Expanding more deeply into the totality of your being, whatever that is, is the aim of meditation. Knowing that nothing is missing, nothing is wrong, and there is nowhere to go, allows us to effortlessly expand beyond the borders of our normal sphere of conscious concern.

I want to be clear that I am not pointing to any need to extend the borders of your normal sphere of conscious concern. Ultimately the expansion of consciousness is not about widening the light of the flashlight beam. It is simply the realization that the light of the flashlight beam and the seeing that it makes available to us, is only part of our experience. Expanding beyond that depends only on knowing that we already have access to experience beyond our normal perceptual habits. We are not expanding our perception, we are realizing a greater awareness that was there all along.

The goal is to be free and being free is not the same as feeling free. When we feel free, it means that we are having some form of conscious experience that we recognize as freedom. Having that experience in our consciousness gives us confidence in the existence of freedom and allows us to let go into the reality of the way things are. For most of us the feeling of freedom is the only thing that alleviates the need to pursue freedom.

Being free means that even if we don't have any particular conscious experience of freedom, we still know that freedom is already here beyond the boundaries of our normal sphere of conscious awareness.

Knowing this allows us to relax into the reality of the way things are without needing to feel free first. We can cease our pursuit of freedom in spite of the fact that no feeling of it can be found in our current conscious experience. This is when we are truly free because our liberation is independent of whether we feel free or not. Feeling free is wonderful, but feeling free is not the same as being free.

The goal is to be free no matter how we feel because that is what freedom is, and that is the only way for us to become truly available for spiritual transformation. Spiritual liberation is spiritual availability. Being free means being available—awake, aware, alert, receptive, and ready—exactly as we are in the world exactly the way it is.

Freedom means being available for life, and we are only available for life when we are no longer preoccupied with needing to feel free. One of the most profound insights I could possibly share with you is that we do not need to have any feeling of freedom in order to be free because free is what we already are.

You road I enter upon and look around, I
  believe you are not all that is here,

I believe that much unseen is also here.

—Walt Whitman

CHAPTER 6

FOURTH INSIGHT:
INTENTION IS NOT WILLPOWER

The final insight that we will be exploring together in this chapter is one that tells us that intention is not willpower. The contemplation of this insight is the key to awakening.

Many of the things we do in life involve willpower. Willpower is the effort it takes to generate change. Willpower is something that you exert over time. The awakening of meditation is not something that can be accomplished with willpower.

Willpower is always associated with effort and effort is always something that involves time. The intention that we are talking about in meditation is not an intention that requires any effort and it is not something that requires any duration of time.

The intention to be free is a choice that happens instantaneously. The intention to be free and the reality of being free, arise simultaneously. There is no gap of time between the intention to be free and the experience of being free.

Just allow yourself to embrace the fact that anything that you might be doing, in the name of being free—that is, anything besides already being free—is not the intention we are talking about.

When we decide to be free, we are deciding to be completely here. We are deciding to have no problem with the way things already are. We are deciding to be content and at peace, no matter what we experience. That intention can only happen instantaneously.

Anything at all that we are doing to try to be free, or to try to be content, or to try to allow things to be the way they already are, is inevitably some form of trying to get somewhere other than here.

The intention to be free is simply a choice to be free that takes no time. Any activity that you place between you and freedom will be some form of insistence on not being free now. It is my experience that everything of real value that can happen during meditation happens only after we have already decided to be free.

Once we have decided to be free, once we have truly let go of making any effort at all to be anywhere other than exactly here, once we have given up trying to change, alter, or manipulate the experience we are having right now, once we are completely surrendered to the way things are, that is when we become truly available for the miraculous—and not a moment before.

Once we let go of the steering wheel, take our feet off the gas and the brake pedal, then are we available and ready for something amazing to happen. Only then can something that is bigger than what we thought we were can take over the driving.

When we make that instantaneous decision to let go and give up control, we are making room for a process of spiritual growth and spiritual evolution to begin within us. This process cannot begin as long as we are trying to control the show, as long as we insist on steering the car ourselves, and as long as we will not take our feet off of the pedals.

But once we have surrendered to the way things are and have given up the struggle to make things different, once we have made that instantaneous choice to let *thy will be done* and not *my* will be done, then we become available for a process that is directed by an intelligent power that is larger than us. At this point we allow our entire being to become fully available for a process of transformation that could never be enacted by any effort of personal willpower.

In the context of meditation, the intention that we are speaking about has nothing to do with making effort. It has nothing to do with maintaining will. It is an intention to surrender. It is surrender. It is an intention to accept wholeheartedly and completely, exactly the way things are. When we do this we become available for something to happen that is beyond us. It is an intentional surrender into a transformative process that opens up inside of us because we have made ourselves available.

We have been taught that freedom means freedom of choice, but that kind of freedom is the freedom of our will. The freedom that I am talking about now is the freedom of availability. It is the freedom that comes when we have finally decided to be completely available for our own spiritual transformation.

It means that we are ready to be transformed and transfigured. We are ready to become something other than what we are. This transformation will never be accomplished through an act of will. It cannot happen through our own effort alone.

The spiritual transformation of our being can only commence when we have given up control and allowed the more subtle energy and intelligence of the profound processes of spiritual evolution to begin to act within us. The choice that we are pointing to is the instantaneous choice to be free, to be surrendered to the way things are, to be available for a process of transformation, and to be vulnerable to the higher energy and wisdom that has been calling and guiding us throughout our whole spiritual journey.

When I sit in deep meditation, surrendered to the way things are, and not in any way attempting to control anything, I feel a deep and delicate process of evolution acting inside me gently, transforming my being.

When I have that experience, I simply allow it to be exactly the way it is. I don't try to control it in any way. I don't try to make it diminish. I don't try to make it increase. I simply allow it to be what it is, not knowing what it is or if it is anything at all.

My experience of that level of surrender to the process of spiritual transformation makes me want to spend as much time as possible in the state of perfect availability, totally at peace and content with everything exactly the way it is. In this state I am available for change, for evolution, and for transformation.

The intention that we work with in meditation is the intention to give up making any effort. It is the intention to unconditionally stop doing anything, and to allow things to be exactly the way they are.

There is no active effort, and no amount of willpower that will ultimately help you do that. It's an intention, and a choice that simultaneously, and instantaneously, leads to the realization that you are already there.

This work does not take a long time to complete for it is the shortest work that one can imagine…it is neither longer or shorter than one impulse of your will, which is the principle active faculty of your soul.

—*The Cloud of Unknowing*

EPILOGUE

THE TRUE VALUE OF SPIRITUAL EXPERIENCE

In my late twenties I stepped out of a fairly traditional life and reassembled myself around a spiritual commitment to a community and a teacher. For twenty years I devoted myself more or less exclusively to spiritual attainment with very little distraction. I devoted my energy during those years to my own ever-deepening awakening, and to mentoring and teaching others. In the space of this epilogue I cannot begin to share the full extent of the spiritual experiences I was blessed with during that time. One of the foundations of my spiritual practice was, and continues to be, meditation, and through that practice I experience energetic openings and spiritual breakthroughs beyond imagination.

I have experienced the sacred grace of having all sense of limitation fall away. This is like realizing that you've been wearing a lead suit all your life, a mental straight jacket made up of all your ideas about what is possible and what is not. In an instant of recognition the constraint and weight simply drop. Suddenly you find yourself blissfully free of limiting beliefs, not knowing what is ultimately possible but compelled by the call of a wide-open future.

During long retreats I have had the opportunity to spend days, weeks, and even months absorbed in meditative unfolding. Many of the awakenings I experienced had the power to dislodge the source of my awareness, allowing me to abide for days in states of consciousness far outside of my habitual sphere of awareness. I have felt energy coursing through my body and white light pouring through the top of my head. I have experienced free-floating awareness that left me completely mystified by my attachment to my mind and body. I have experienced the pure awareness that I was before I was born, will be after I die, and is even now the ultimate source of my being.

Eventually it became clear that having one more spiritual experience would not make any difference. I had already had more awakenings than I could remember and I was beyond the point of needing any additional evidence.

Having experiences is not the goal. None of them matter in and of themselves. Their gift is that they awaken a deep appreciation for the enormity of reality. They attest to the fact that we will never be able to capture the mystery of our being in our minds. Knowing this leaves us wide open, receptive, and available for whatever is next.

I am left with the firm conviction that reality will always be bigger than we can imagine. We are not restricted by the limits and boundaries of our minds and bodies. And as long as we continue to surrender, the openings and awakenings of spirit will ceaselessly unfold to illuminate the way forward.

There is no end to the mysteries of the inner life.

There is always more mystery.

—Anaïs Nin

ABOUT THE AUTHOR

Jeff Carreira originally received an undergraduate degree in physics and spent five years working as a research engineer before realizing that life's deepest questions could not be answered through science alone. He decided to work in a more humanitarian field and received a master's degree in education and spent seven years working as a special-education teacher and school administrator.

He embarked on a life devoted to awakening in 1992 when he met spiritual teacher Andrew Cohen and embraced the perspective of Evolutionary Enlightenment. A series of life-changing experiences led him to become a prominent member of a global spiritual movement where he created educational programs that supported the ongoing spiritual growth of people around the world.

Currently he teaches with Patricia Albere co-leading the Evolutionary Collective. In their collaborative work they explore the transformative possibilities of a higher order of human relatedness. Together they support the growth and development of an international community of people who are committed to living on the emerging edge of Spirit's unfolding.

Jeff is the author of three books, *The Miracle of Meditation, Philosophy Is Not a Luxury,* and *Radical Inclusivity,* and is co-author with Patricia Albere of *Mutual Awakening.* For more information about Jeff visit:

www.jeffcarreira.com

Made in the USA
Middletown, DE
12 January 2017